CHRISTMAS TREASURES OF THE HEART

by

Cheri Fuller

HONOR BOOKS

Tulsa, Oklahoma

Unless otherwise indicated, all Scripture quotations are taken from the *King James Version* of the Bible.

Scripture quotations marked NAS are taken from the *New American Standard Bible*. Copyright © The Lockman Foundation, 1960, 1962, 1963, 1968, 1971, 1972, 1973, 1975, 1977. Used by permission.

Verses marked TLB are taken from The Living Bible Company © 1971. Used by permission of Tyndale House Publishers, Inc., Wheaton, Illinois 60189. All rights reserved.

Christmas Treasures of the Heart
ISBN 1-56292-149-5
Copyright © 1995 by Cheri Fuller
P. O. Box 770493
Oklahoma City, Oklahoma 73177

Published by Honor Books, Inc.
P. O. Box 55388
Tulsa, Oklahoma 74155-1388

CONTENTS

A Note to Readers &
Lovers of Christmas

What are holiday traditions? Customary ways of doing things, yes — but Christmas traditions are much more. They are "treasures of the heart," activities, food or family rituals that we enjoy together in the present but remember fondly for years to come. In fact, holiday traditions are part of a quilt of memories that reach all the way back to our childhoods.

Whether making a new Christmas tree ornament each year, caroling to neighbors, constructing a gingerbread house, or putting a candle in each window, traditions are an important way to build a sense of continuity and security. Traditions say, "This is who we are, and what we hold dear as a family." They help make up the glue that holds families together. In times of moving, loss, and the changes that life brings, they provide a sense of belonging for children and offer an opportunity to pass on to them our values like kindness, unselfishness, generosity, and love for others.

"How do we keep our balance?" asks Tevye, the Jewish dairyman in the beloved musical play *Fiddler on the Roof*.

"Tradition!" he rightly concludes. "Without tradition, our lives would be as shaky as a fiddler on a roof."

So too in our day, traditions help us keep our balance. In a world of ceaseless mobility, constant uncertainty, and change, traditions serve to steady our lives and keep us on course. The family Christmas pie prepared year after year, customs handed down from past generations, sharing Christmas Eve with friends and family in our own special way. All these traditions — old and new — weave our lives together into a tapestry of memories that will last for a lifetime.

> *Create a Quilt of Memories*
> *to keep me warm.*
> *An inner warmth that comes*
> *from light of happy times.*
> *Weave in the threads of holidays,*
> *of friends and families...*
> *Delights of seashore, fields,*
> *of city parks.*
> *The simplest happenings*
> *traced out in love*
> *become a pattern,*
> *for my quilt of memories.[1]*
>
> **— Ruth Reardon**

Enjoying This Holiday Book

This book contains many activities and ideas which are "memory-makers." That doesn't mean that you should try to make all the memories or do all of the activities this holiday season! It can be a resource for Christmases to come, also.

- Enjoy it section by section, taking time for each heartwarming story, poem, or legend during the Advent or "pre-Christmas" days. For example, as you read about the origin of stockings in holiday celebrations one week, try doing one of the suggested crafts after you read the story to your child or get out rhythm instruments and sing the carol. On another week, try the recipe for Make-Ahead Cranberry Bread. If there are three Christmas activities, choose one.

- If an activity strikes you as something your family would enjoy, jot it down and adapt it to your existing traditions. If your schedule is too full, circle it, and save it for next year's celebration.

- Be open to new customs. Traditions are formed delicately, sometimes without our realizing it. If an experience or activity you try brings joy this holiday, you may want to repeat it next year. We can be the "keeper of traditions," but also flexible and sensitive to the needs of family members, willing to make changes or try something new.

CHAPTER ONE

Christmas Is Coming

*D*eck the halls, prepare the house for Advent, for CHRISTMAS IS COMING! Advent means "arrival" or "coming." It is the time on the calendar that begins four Sundays before Christmas and ends on Christmas Day. Advent has been celebrated by churches for centuries as a time of meditation, prayer, and waiting for the birth of Christ. It is a time for making room for Him in our hearts and homes. To help us prepare for Christmas, Advent wreaths, calendars, and activities have come into being. Families decorate houses and Christmas trees, make gifts, and prepare cards to send.

> *Christmas Is Coming!*
> *Christmas…the season of gifts great and small when joy is the nicest gift of them all.*
> —Anonymous

Candlelight Dinner

*O*nce each week in December, light a group of candles in candleholders in the middle of the table for the evening meal. (See next page for an easy-to-make special main dish for your candlelight dinner!) Turn out the lights and enjoy the warmth of the candlelight. Go around the table and share a happy memory from holidays past or something each person is grateful for. After eating, stay around the candlelit table and have someone read a Christmas story or legend. There are many throughout this book to pick from!

The spirit of Christmas brings memories drifting down like snowflakes.
— Dorothy Colgan

Holiday Chicken

*T*o make creamed chicken: In a crock pot or dutch oven, put 5 or 6 boneless skinless chicken breasts, a large can of cream of chicken soup, 1/2 cup milk, and a large can of chicken broth; cook on low until done.

- Prepare ahead enough servings of rice for your family.

- Prepare toppings in individual bowls: pineapple chunks, chopped celery, coconut, slivered almonds, grated cheese, Chinese crunchy noodles, chopped scallions, diced tomatoes or red bell peppers (plus your personal favorite topping).

- Arrange bowls of toppings around the candles in the center of the table.

- To serve, pour creamed chicken and gravy over the rice, and let each person embellish with desired toppings. Delicious, colorful, and easy to prepare!

Serve with a large loaf of French bread and a green salad, and you have a special meal for the family and even company.

A Family Welcome Wreath

*T*ake a green wreath and decorate it with whatever characterizes the special memories and interests of each family member during the past year: a Scout badge, a small ballet shoe, a memento from a campout trip, a tiny bride and groom to recall a family wedding. With florist wire and picks, attach these items to the wreath, and weave bright thin ribbon in and out in a festive way. (It is simplest to buy the wreath and "make" it your own with your mementoes, ribbons, and decorations.)

Hang the wreath on your front door to welcome all who come

in during the holiday season. Then after Christmas, cover the wreath with a big clear plastic sack, and save it as a "snapshot" of your year, a little bit of history.

CHAPTER TWO

Christmas Is For Giving

We Three Kings of Orient Are

We three kings of Orient are,
Bearing gifts we traverse afar,
Field and fountain, moor and mountain,
Following yonder star.

Refrain: O Star of wonder, star of night,
Star with royal beauty bright,
Westward leading, still proceeding,
Guide us to thy perfect light.

Born a King on Bethlehem's plain,
Gold I bring to crown Him again,
King forever, ceasing never
Over us all to reign.

Refrain.   — John Henry Hopkins, Jr.

The Christmas Seashell

Long ago one Christmas in an African village, school was letting out for the holiday. A shy little boy came up to the desk and presented his missionary-teacher with a beautiful seashell as a Christmas present. The boy had walked many, many miles to a special inlet of the ocean, the only place such a shell could be found. "How wonderful that you have traveled so far for this lovely present," said the teacher, greatly touched by his gift. At once the boy's eyes brightened as he said, "Long walk part of gift."

As you make and wrap gifts and prepare for Christmas, remember that the preparation you make for family and friends — the baking, the wrapping, and looking for just the right present — is all part of your gift to them.

Christmas On a Shoestring

It was two weeks before Christmas and a sudden business reversal had left the Morris family with barely enough to pay the house payment and utilities. As she looked in the checkbook, Cynthia was grateful the necessities were covered. But her heart sank as she gazed over at the tree and realized there was no money left for Christmas gifts. Having made a pledge to avoid any credit-card buying that year, Cynthia pondered what she and her husband would do for their four children and their giving to each other. One of the favorite parts of the kids' Christmas had been buying little gifts for their parents and each other.

That night she and Dave sat down with their children and announced, "This year we're doing something different. If we give gifts to each other, we'll make them, but only from supplies around the house — nothing store-bought."

Each person went about their household chores and homework, but all the time thinking of what could be made. A few days later David, while at a friend's house, shared the different way his family was handling gift-giving, and said how much he wanted to make something special for his mom. Tommy's mom produced an old wooden recipe box, and David found moss, shells, and seeds to glue on and decorate for his mother. The sisters made packs of coupons for services: "Mom, I will do the dishes for you on your night cheerfully." "This coupon is good for three foot rubs for you, Dad."

As the homemade gifts and coupons were opened by the family on Christmas morning, joy filled the home. The girls were thrilled with the coupon Dad had wrapped up promising six hours of work restoring their doll house. Caroline had made special cookies for everyone. Mom was thrilled with her new recipe box. The little love gifts — gifts of time from the heart — gave them more joy than big gifts ever had, and helped them focus on the real meaning of Christmas — the birth of Christ and serving one another and others outside the family. The children are almost grown now, but looking back, it was the best Christmas ever, the one they will never forget.

Christmas Coupons

*E*ach family member gives a coupon to the others with a promised service (like cleaning, vacuuming, snow shoveling) or a time to look forward to spending together (a day at the military museum with Dad or a day at the zoo and picnic with Mom).

For parents, a special coupon gift is lessons, teaching your child something new that you're an "expert" in. One dad gave his teenage son lessons in computer programming. A mom gave her daughter a promised twelve hours of sewing lessons. In any case, the fun of doing or learning something together lasts long after the holiday.

You could give a friend a coupon saying: "I'll make and deliver a dessert next time you have company" or "I'll keep your children for one weekend while you have a break or little trip."

Make the Christmas coupons on blank white index cards, and decorate with stickers or colorful marker-art. Put them in an envelope and place in the recipients' Christmas stockings. As the gifts are "redeemed" and enjoyed, Christmas lasts all year.

Keeping Christmas All Year Long
(and Preventing Holiday Stress)

- During the year, write down gift ideas when they come to you.

- If you find the perfect gift in July or any other month, purchase it.

- Look for stocking stuffers at department, discount, and drug store close-outs.

- Store your newfound treasures in a "Secret Santa" drawer.

- When the holidays come, you won't be shopping as frantically; you'll be glad to have a treasure chest of thoughtful gifts to draw from.

> *"I will honour Christmas in my heart, and try to keep it all the year."*
> — Ebenezer Scrooge, *A Christmas Carol* by Charles Dickens

Baking Tips for Christmas Kitchens

- Buy a few sacks of fresh cranberries before Thanksgiving when they are plentiful, and freeze them for holiday baking.

- Collect baking tins and baskets in after-holiday sales and garage sales all year round to use for giving gifts from your kitchen.

- Keep your ground spices tightly stored so that air and heat won't dull the taste and smell. After a year, throw them away!

- Make up extra sugar cookie dough and freeze in frozen juice cans. Then push out, slice, decorate, and bake when unexpected friends drop by during the holidays or any time you need fresh cookies.

- Flour your cookie cutters and molds before using so the dough won't stick.

- Since all baking products — flour, sugar, etc. — are cheaper at holiday time, stock up for your year-round baking needs, and you'll save money!

Sharing the Joy

Extend kindness toward newcomers in your neighborhood or church this Christmas season. People who have recently moved feel especially lonely during the holidays. Having left behind friends and family, they have also lost familiar surroundings and holiday activities. In the new place, they do not know about community events and are often not invited to Christmas parties. It means so much to be included in the holiday festivities of the new area! You can build a bridge of friendship and make a difference in someone's first Christmas in town by:

> *You never really leave a place you love. Part of it you take with you, leaving a part of you behind.*
> — Anonymous

- Inviting a new neighbor to a school Christmas play or holiday event in the community or at your church.

- Inviting a new family to your home for a meal in December.

- Taking a plate of cookies or Christmas cranberry bread to newcomers.

CHAPTER THREE

Angels Among Us

$\mathcal{A}$ngels have had an important place in the Christmas season ever since the first Christmas. Silver angels are traditional Christmas tree-toppers, gleaming glass angels decorate the branches, little clay angels hold candles and appear in nativity scenes. Most important, angels symbolize the Christmas message of peace and good will. Angels announce the Good News!

Luke's account tells us how the angel of the Lord appeared to "the shepherds keeping watch over their flocks by night," and brought them "good tidings of great joy," announcing the birth of the Christ Child. Then a host of angels proclaimed, "Glory to God in the highest, and on earth peace, good will toward men!"

Make a
Clay Christmas Angel
for Your Tree

Following the salt-dough recipe in Chapter 4, roll out the dough, and using an angel cookie cutter, cut out the shape. Make a hole with the point of a pencil for the hanger or ribbon. Make hair for the angel by pushing the dough through a garlic press; then moisten and attach. Paint with acrylics. After completely dry, spray with glossy acrylic and hang on your tree.

The shepherds had an angel
The wise men had a star;
But what have I,
a little child,
To guide me home from far
Where glad stars
sing together,
And singing angels are?
— **Christina Rossetti**

Four Ways To Get Your Wings
— Be an Angel and...

- Give someone a little gift that meets a need, and do it anonymously.

- When other family members are occupied, do their job or responsibility without asking for thanks.

- Write a kind, encouraging note to someone you know needs a lift.

- Visit a shut-in. Take tea bags and cookies for a "cup of Christmas tea" to enjoy together, and bring along your favorite Christmas book. Read a story or two aloud. Ask your friend to share about her fondest memories of Christmases past. If she has written a few cards or letters, offer to mail them.

*How grand and how bright
That wonderful night
When angels to
Bethlehem came,
They burst forth like fires
They struck their gold lyres
And mingled their sound
with the flame.*
— **Seventeenth-century English carol**

The Angel and the Helicopter

"What are we going to pray for tonight, Jay?" I asked as I knelt by my son's bed a few weeks before Christmas. It might be for his brother who was away at college, or for his grandparents. But tonight Jay requested an angel. Sometimes it's difficult to understand Jay because of a speech disorder, but with sign language and gestures he eventually gets his message across.

Jay was born with Down's syndrome and severe congenital heart disease. Now, at 17, the heart disease was progressing rapidly. In an effort to protect his health we schooled Jay at home. But tonight was his first night on oxygen, and he was frightened. He wanted an angel. As I prayed, my mind raced back to a day weeks earlier when Jay had told me about seeing an angel in his room.

"What did he look like?" I asked.

He wiggled his thumb and pinkie and signed, "Yellow."

"You mean the angel's clothes were yellow?"

"Yeah."

"What color was his hair?"

"Yellow."

"What about his face?"

Again the thumb and pinkie said, "Yellow."

"Everything about him was yellow?"

Suddenly I realized that Jay had no way of saying golden, bright, or shining, so his description made sense. My son had seen an angel!

Soon Jay began to tolerate the oxygen but his prayer request remained the same — an angel. And each time he looked toward the door and smiled. Finally, I had to ask, "Jay, do you see an angel?"

"Yeah!"

"Where?" I looked at the end of the bed thinking that was where a guardian angel should be.

Jay motioned with his hand. "The door." Patiently, he explained that an angel stood there every night and sometimes spoke to him.

During this time I also prayed for a special friend for Jay. He missed having classmates. Jay needs a friend, I told God often, someone to talk to, a buddy to play army with. He prized his collection of G.I. Joe figures, tanks, and helicopters, and it broke my heart to see him playing with them alone for hours. Of course, each night we continued to pray for angels.

One night a grinding noise and white light came alive in the corner. Startled, I jumped onto Jay's bed! He laughed and pointed to a helicopter on his dresser. Its lights and propeller were activated by pressing a button; but how had the crazy thing turned itself on? Another time I found a remote-controlled army tank rolling across Jay's floor at 2 a.m., its red light flashing in the dark while Jay slept peacefully. My husband explained it away as having "something to do with radio waves." But who pushed the button on the helicopter?

In the days ahead I came to believe that God had sent a wonderful gift — an angel who liked G.I. Joe tanks and helicopters. I also realized that Jay now had his special friend. I can't see him, but Jay can. He doesn't speak to me, but he talks to Jay. Every night I pray for this angel and I feel his presence. In fact, some nights when I'm extremely concerned about Jay's health, I stop at the door and ask this unseen warrior to stay especially close to my son while he sleeps.

What a gracious and loving heavenly Father to let a lonesome and frightened young man become friends with his guardian angel. And what reassurance for me to know that one day this mighty angel will carry him to Heaven. In fact, who knows, they just might make the trip by helicopter!

— Louise Tucker Jones

Our Littlest Angels

Babies and young children are a joy and a challenge, but especially at Christmas we appreciate the wonder with which they approach each day. Here's a way to remind everyone of the special "Baby's First Christmas":

- Baby Shoe Ornaments: Gather one baby shoe for each child in the family. On the bottom of each shoe, write in gold or silver paint the name and birth date of the family member.

- Photo Ornaments: Take a metal lid from an orange juice can. Spray the lid red, green, or gold. Cut a photo of the child to fit inside the "frame." Then poke a hole through the lid with an ice pick. String green crochet thread through the hole, and — voilà! — a framed ornament. Make one each year for each child and you build a little gallery of precious memories.

Christmas Is For Kids

What better way to make happy memories and start the holidays when school lets out than with a party for neighborhood children? You supply treats and materials for them to decorate jolly gingerbread people (which they get to take home) or "make-and-take" a gift for parents. Tasting is permissible, accompanied by warm apple cider simmered with a few cinnamon sticks!

Old Fashioned Gingerbread People

Ingredients:
1/4 cup butter (at room temperature)
1/2 cup molasses
1 teaspoon baking soda, cinnamon,
    and ginger
1/2 teaspoon salt
1/2 cup light brown sugar
3 1/2 cups flour
1/4 teaspoon nutmeg
1/3 cup water

Directions:

For making gingerbread people: To make the cookies before the kids arrive, blend the butter and brown sugar in a big bowl until creamy. Beat in molasses. Sift all dry ingredients together in another bowl. Add the dry mixture to the wet in thirds, alternating with the water. Blend, and then knead lightly with floured hands. Form dough into a ball, cover with waxed paper, and refrigerate for 3 to 4 hours.

Preheat oven to 350 degree F; roll out dough to 1/4 inch thickness. Cut cookies into gingerbread people shapes. Bake for 12 minutes or until done. Cool and decorate.

For decorating: Provide small tubes of colored icing, red hots or M & Ms, and raisins. Cover table with vinyl cloth and plenty of wax paper for spills, and HAVE FUN! To make a gingerbread ornament, you can carefully punch a hole in the top of the cookie with an ice pick before baking. Then when cool, decorate and spray with acrylic fixative. If you don't have time to make dough, buy plain store-bought gingerbread men; the children will have just as much fun decorating them!

*Gently teach us
how to find
Joy and trust in
one another —
Lasting faith in
all mankind.*
— Anonymous

TIP: Insert a lollipop stick into gingerbread cookies before baking and when cool, frost and decorate. Enclose in clear plastic wrap and tie with ribbon around the stick for a festive look.

Fill Your Home With Pretty Sights...
Santa Apples

- Take one apple, shined with Crisco, for Santa's body. Place it upside-down on waxed paper.

- Stick 3 or 4 cranberries on toothpicks for the legs and arms. (Allow the arms to angle in a slight "V" and the legs to come a bit forward.)

- Place one toothpick in the back as a prop to help Santa stand.

- Use whole, fresh cloves for Santa's eyes, nose, mouth, and the buttons down the front of his suit.

- Attach cotton with glue for Santa's beard, coming to a point.

- Create Santa's head from one large marshmallow, and his hat from one cranberry. (This Santa is for looking, not eating!)[2]

The Santa Letter

Write special letters of appreciation and love in each stocking. Include little reminders of the past year like how proud you are of progress your child has made or a character quality you've seen developing.

Write on decorative paper (which can be purchased by the sheet at copy shops), or make a holiday border around the letter. Enclose in an envelope, and the Santa letter will become one of the favorite "stocking stuffers" at your house.

TIP: While looking for stocking stuffers and gifts, wrap a small gift in silver and gold for each person, to be opened only when the tree ornaments are put away and the tree taken up to the attic or to the curb. These "Twelfth Night" gifts, from the Wise Men, will encourage your helpers so you won't be stuck with dismantling the tree by yourself.

CHAPTER FOUR

O Christmas Tree

Get out any instrument you have (guitar, piano, recorder) and give your children rhythm instruments or make them:

Shakers: put rice in a small plastic container with a tight lid. An empty medicine container works well. Attach the lid securely with masking tape.

Drums: take a round oatmeal or other hot cereal container and decorate it with construction paper, cut and taped to fit.

Clackers: create from two wooden spoons.

Then let everyone enjoy playing along with the beat and singing together:

One Starry Night

 $\mathcal{H}$ istory tells us that five hundred years ago Martin Luther, German leader of the Protestant Reformation, began the custom of decorating Christmas trees.

While walking through the woods one beautiful starry night near Christmas Eve, Luther gazed at a large evergreen tree illuminated by the starlight. He was struck by the beautiful sight which reminded him of the night the angels appeared to the shepherds in Bethlehem announcing the birth of the Christ Child. He cut down a small pine tree and brought it home. There Luther decorated the tree with lighted candles which he told his wife and children represented Christ as the Light of the World. From that small beginning, the popular custom of decorating trees quickly spread throughout Europe and later to America. Early trees were also decorated with small candies, cookies, paper, and glass ornaments.

Carefully picked and trimmed with tiny twinkling lights —
festooned with ornaments made by our children and us, ornaments
from friends in Germany and across the country, as well as those
collected during our travels — our family Christmas tree is more
than just a decoration in the living room; it's full of Christmas
memories and shines forth as a symbol of love and friendship.

Christmas Tree Safety Tips

- After you get the tree home, recut the base before placing the tree in water.

- Hang a few bells around the bottom of the tree so you'll hear when your pet's paws or little one's hands are in the decorations.

- Use only lights with the approved UL (safety-tested) label.

- Plug no more than three sets of lights in a series into one socket.

- Place breakable or glass ornaments on deep inside branches.

- When you go away from your home, or are asleep, turn off all lights, including the tree lights!

Tree Trimming Night

In our family we serve the same kind of treats each year on the tree-trimming night, and the children look forward to it. Our favorite is hot cocoa or cider with cookies. That's the first night we get out our holiday music tapes from years past — like "The Nutcracker Suite," and "Music Box Christmas" — and play the music, singing along while decorating the tree and throughout the month.

Every year on this evening, each child is presented with an ornament, either purchased or hand-made, to hang on the tree, and has a small box with his or her name on it in which to keep the growing collection of shiny baubles. When the children are grown and begin their own households, the ornaments will go with them to trim their own family trees.

Share the Fun of Tree Decorating:

- If you're empty nesters, invite a couple with young children to help you decorate.

- Invite a few singles from your community or church to join you.

- Then share a big pot of steaming soup and French bread with your friends, after the tree decorating is complete.

The Christmas Hot Chocolate

"*N*o hot chocolate on Christmas Eve?" our teenage daughter, Christine, asked. I looked away. "Next year," I promised as she went to get ready for the midnight service.

We'd always had hot chocolate on Christmas Eve; it was a family tradition. But this year we couldn't afford even that simple item. When my husband, Jack, was laid off six months earlier, he started a claims-adjusting business, working out of our basement. But the response had been dreadful, and it didn't help when our car's transmission died. Our older daughter, Janice, contributed her earnings from her first full-time job, and the girls never complained about doing without. Still, as the year drew to a close, our financial picture looked bleaker and bleaker.

As we headed out the door, my eyes fell on our old artificial tree draped with last year's dulled tinsel. And I couldn't even squeeze money for hot chocolate out of our budget, I thought. During the service I prayed silently, Oh, Lord, you promised to take care of us. Have you forgotten?

Everyone except me, it seemed, was uplifted by the message of hope in the service. At its close, people hugged and shook hands. As we bundled up in coats and scarves, Christine's youth counselor called to us: "Wait!" She pulled a ribboned jar from her bag. "Merry Christmas!" She had brought us hot chocolate mix!

She hadn't known about our family tradition. And she didn't know that, to me, this simple gift was a reminder that God had not forgotten us after all.[3]

— Cheryl Morrison

Hand-Made Ornaments

The first year my husband and I were married, we had no room in our budget for buying ornaments, so a friend and I bought styrofoam balls at the dime store and covered them with strips of red and green gingham, braid, and ribbon. With shiny red bows tied on its branches, we thought it made the prettiest tree ever.

So we have continued to make Christmas tree decorations through the years: cross-stitched Santas, salt-dough stars, felt snowmen, silver balls with names spelled out in glitter, lacy paper, glittered snowflakes, and painted rocking horses. Making ornaments is a good way to involve children in the spirit of Christmas and to have fun together.

In a survey, thousands of school children were asked what they thought makes a happy family. The kids didn't answer a big house, designer jeans, or CD players. The most-mentioned key to happiness was DOING THINGS TOGETHER.

Lacy Paper Snowflakes

Materials: Several sheets of thin white (silver or gold) paper, sharp scissors, and strong string.

Directions: Fold a square of paper into eighths. Make random cuts in the paper, some straight and some curved, some deep and others shallow. When the paper is unfolded, you can add a dash of silver glitter to the edges of the snowflakes.

Suspended on the branches of a tree by a string loop, these paper snowflakes add a homey, old-fashioned touch.

Rudolph the Red-Nosed Reindeer Candy Cane Ornaments

Materials:

Candy canes

Pipe cleaners, 2 per reindeer

Plastic wiggle eyes, size to scale — 2 per reindeer

Small red pompoms, to scale with candy cane — 1 per reindeer

Narrow red ribbon

Scissors and tacky craft glue

Directions for each ornament:

- Twist one pipe cleaner around the curve in the candy cane.

- Cut the other pipe cleaner in half. Twist the short pieces of the pipe cleaner around the end of the long pipe cleaner. Turn up the ends of the stems and bend to look like antlers.

- With white glue, attach two small (7 mm.) wiggle eyes and a small red pom-pom nose to the end of the curved candy cane.

- To hang Rudolph from the tree, tie a thin red ribbon around the curve of the candy cane. Rudolph is also a happy favor for a kids' holiday party, a favorite teacher, or a special package decoration.

Salt-Dough Christmas Stars

Ingredients:
4 cups flour
1 cup salt
1 1/2 cups hot tap water

Directions: Mix and knead the dough until it is smooth and pliable. If too sticky, work in a little more flour. If the dough is too dry, moisten your fingers with water and knead a bit longer. Roll out the dough to about an inch thick. Use cookie cutters in the shapes of stars, bells, angels, Santas, or whatever patterns you have on hand. You can also use your imagination to shape wreaths, candy canes, etc. With a garlic press, push dough through to make hair; then moisten it and stick on the ornament.

With the point of a pencil, punch a hole for a string or thin ribbon hanger.

Bake at 350 degrees F until hardened. If air bubbles start to form while baking, prick ornament with a needle. When cool, use acrylic paints to fill in the figures with color. Then after drying completely, spray with a glossy or matte acrylic to apply final finish.

O star of wonder, star of night, Star with royal beauty bright, Westward leading, still proceeding Guide us to thy perfect light.
— **"We Three Kings of Orient Are"**

Unlikely Places

In 1975 our four-year-old son Justin was in the hospital recovering from a severe asthma attack. We had planned to spend a traditional family Christmas at home, but as it turned out our young son was one of the few patients in the children's ward who was just too ill to be released. Despite our carefully laid plans, it was clear we would not be home for the holidays.

The whole hospital experience had been painful — for Justin and for me. I felt sorry for him, for instead of sitting on Santa's knee sharing his Christmas wish, or hanging his stocking on the mantelpiece, there he was on Christmas Eve day — stuck in a drab hospital, hooked up to an IV, and caged by an oxygen tent.

With no friends in town since we were newcomers, the hospital was a lonely place to be at Christmas time. I was disappointed that my own last-minute plans for cookie-baking and package-wrapping had been spoiled. And I missed our eighteen-month-old son Chris who was at home with Dad in our family room which, when we left for the hospital, had been all aglow with twinkling lights, gaily colored felt stockings all hung in a row, and shining candles.

Justin and I gazed for hours at monotonous grey walls, faded cowboy curtains, and drab construction-paper bells left over from Christmases past. I felt angry and frustrated, yet didn't want to show it. I needed to help keep Justin's spirits up until we could get him back home. My husband's family had decided we would all postpone Christmas until the day Justin returned home from the hospital. Until then, they said, we would act as if Christmas hadn't yet arrived.

While we had expected to put off Christmas, God had other plans, and was to use this experience to teach us the true meaning of Christmas.

On Christmas Eve, a man brightly dressed as Santa Claus came bounding down the hall and delivered a cowboy hat, just his size, to Justin. As I watched him continue down the hall delivering presents, I asked the nurse, "Did some organization send this gift as a yearly project?"

"Oh, no," she replied. "Three years ago a mom and dad's only daughter, three years old, died in this ward on Christmas Eve. Now each year the parents find out the exact size or need of each child, and have the gifts delivered by Santa so they can remain anonymous. They know what it's like to be here."

While I was pondering this act of kindness, two little Campfire girls brought in a hand-made white felt mitten ornament decorated with holly, and presented it to Justin. "Merry Christmas!" they chimed as they continued happily down the hall.

Hardly had their words faded away when a family of Mexican-American carolers arrived. Gaily dressed in red and green native costumes, guitars in hand, they sang to us of the "Silent Night" and concluded their carol-singing with "Joy to the World." And we were going to "put off Christmas"!

Next, a big University of Oklahoma football player in his varsity jersey strolled in and began to chat with Justin. An avid football fan, Justin couldn't believe that a "real live" gridiron hero had come just to see him. He was all the more amazed and delighted when the burly athlete produced a surprise gift for him.

"A cowboy rifle and spurs!" he exclaimed. "They go with the hat!"

The coincidence took my breath away.

The next day, on Christmas morning, a tall, thin, shabbily dressed man quietly entered the room and sat on the edge of Justin's bed. Like some character from a Dickens' novel, his clothes were tattered and worn. Without a word, he took out an old flute and began to play a lovely Christmas medley. One carol blended into another as the simplicity of each song took on a beauty beyond any I had ever known. Finishing his serenade like the little drummer boy, he handed Justin a small cup full of tiny red candies. Then with a smile, he slipped out the door.

Slowly, but clearly, I began to realize that none of the people who had shared their love and gifts with us knew us or had even told us their names. We had done nothing to earn or deserve their gifts.

While my own hurts from the past had created a cold barrier around my heart, these simple acts of kindness had caused the walls of neglected feelings to come tumbling down.

That lonely hospital, with its drab walls lined with construction-paper bells, had become a place of God's healing and reconciling love. Away from family, friends, and our baby son, without our tree or traditions, God had delivered to us His special Christmas gift. The loneliest and darkest of places had been filled with the presence of angels and the brightest of lights.

> *No act of kindness, no matter how small, is ever wasted.*
> — **Aesop**

A Christmas Photo Album

The Christmas album is a special place to keep all of your Christmas keepsake photographs so you don't have to wonder each year, "Where is the photo of the children sitting on Santa's knee that year we had just moved here?" or "Where's that picture of Granddad setting up the train set?"

Every year at our house we get out the green satin-covered Christmas album and place it on the coffee table. The album's pages begin with a few old pictures of my husband and me under our own childhood Christmas trees, our first Christmas as newlyweds, the children's first Christmases, and so on through the years. Photos include school plays, friends who joined us for holiday gatherings, tree-trimming nights, and special events.

No matter how busy the family members are or how "grownup" our children become, we all spend some time perusing the Christmas album each holiday season.

To make your Christmas album:

- Take a standard or large photo album.

- Cover the album in a bright holiday fabric — red, green, country print, or fancy satin. Embroider by stitching the word "Christmas" diagonally across the cover by hand or machine (or take it to a monogram shop) before placing it on the album.

- Add to the fun by inserting holiday photos right after Christmas, before they get stuck in a cabinet drawer somewhere!

If we think of our heart, rather than our purse, as the reservoir of our giving, we shall find it full all the time!
— **David Dunn**

TIP: When friends and family include a photo with their Christmas card, have a special "Friends and Family" bulletin board to post them on and enjoy them year round.

CHAPTER FIVE

Sharing Good Tidings of Great Joy

Christmas Cards

Christmas wouldn't be the same
If we couldn't get in touch
With all the friends and family
Who mean so very much.

— Anonymous

Christmas Card & Photo Tips

- Shop after-Christmas sales for great bargains on Christmas cards.

- Aim for September or October for your family photo to be snapped. Dress everyone in similar or coordinating colors (all in denim shirts, or red and green sweaters, for example). You could even snap the picture at a summer reunion or family outing.

- After choosing the best photo, have it duplicated before October 31, when most photo shops are offering special discounts.

- Gather around a lovely tree outdoors, in front of a wreath or sitting on different levels of stools and chairs around the fireplace.

The Christmas Card Custom

For me and many other people, writing and sending cards is as much a part of Christmas as decorating the tree! Long ago, there were no commercial Christmas cards available to purchase. People wrote personal notes wishing their friends good cheer and a prosperous and happy new year. In the nineteenth century, British schoolboys were required to write in fancy calligraphy and decorate holiday greetings on elaborate scrolls. In 1843 the first Christmas card was designed, illustrated, and printed by lithography. The elaborate cards were then hand-colored and sold. Other printers caught the idea, and soon thousands of cards were being produced and printed in England and the United States.

While some people have their name embossed on the cards, others prefer to handwrite a greeting with their name. Many families enclose a photo of the whole group, the children, or even a favorite pet. Ambitious folks write an annual "Christmas letter" copied on red, green, or bordered paper — as a way of keeping in touch with friends and family and expressing their own "Merry Christmas"!

TIP: Whether you buy or make Christmas cards to send, or write a family Christmas letter, save a copy of each year's greeting (and photo, if you included one.) Put them in an album. Your children and grandchildren will someday love walking down the holiday lane of memories through your Christmas cards.

Audio & Video Greetings

Sending "good tidings of great joy" to family and friends doesn't have to be limited to printed cards. With Christmas cassette greetings, you purchase a blank cassette tape, put it in your player, and start recording! These easy-to-create holiday greetings can include: the family singing carols, each person sharing personal news, readings of favorite Christmas stories and poems. Add one of your kid playing his first carols on the piano or other musical instrument, and one last "Merry Christmas!" and your cassette is complete.

With a current photo of the family, Grandpa, Grandma, or the recipient will feel like he or she has had a warm, cheerful visit.

You can also create a lively video greeting if you have a video camera, to reach out and bring loved ones closer together in heart, if not in miles. Once when we were two thousand miles away from home at holiday time, I borrowed a video camera and made a recorded Christmas greeting to send to family — complete with shots of our tree, a school musical performance our children participated in, caroling across-the-miles as we sang favorite Christmas songs. Then I interviewed each family member so he or she could share personal news flashes and individual holiday wishes.

You could even film your children acting out a simple nativity play with home-made costumes. Put your heads together, have one person act as "director" of the Christmas video, and have a ball.

The Joy of Christmas Cards—
What To Do With the Ones You Receive

- When Christmas cards begin arriving, put them in a ribbon-bedecked basket on the dinner table. As you gather for meals, read a card or two aloud. That way you can enjoy the cards and keep loved ones and friends in mind all through the month of December, and even into January.

- Keep double-sided masking tape in a drawer in the kitchen, and as cards come in the mail each day or so, have your child stick them on a door in a Christmas shape (tree, angel, or star).

- Hang strong cord or kite string across a wall or side of a room and when cards come, hang the colorful cards to make a bright, cheerful garland that stretches across the family or play room.

Creating the
Family Christmas Newsletter

*O*ne of my favorite traditions at Christmas time is the writing and sending of our family newsletter. My main purpose is to keep in touch with friends and family members far away, especially elderly ones who look forward to hearing about the graduation of their great-grandson, school news of the grandchildren, and other events.

To me, one of the best things about writing newsletters is the family history that is slowly forming. I have a file of these "annual reports" and add a copy of the new Christmas message each year.

TIME-SAVING TIP: If you don't have time and money to send individual cards, compose a Christmas greeting in rhyme or other jolly format on your computer, and then e-mail it to all your relatives and

> *There's nothing like greeting Good friends, new and old, To give holiday hours All the warmth they can hold!*
> — **Anonymous**

friends who are "tele-computing!" You compose the message, then with the click of a key, individual electronic mail messages are sent to many people almost instantaneously.

Family Christmas Newsletter Directions

*H*ere are some tips for putting together a family newsletter of your own:

- Around Thanksgiving start thinking about the letter and ask other family members for ideas: "What do we want to include in our Christmas letter this year?" "What are some of the special highlights of the past twelve months?"

- Organize your material: you can write it month-by-month, highlighting the important happenings in your journey through the year, or have a "frame" (for example, one friend wrote a humorous holiday letter from the perspective of the family dog).

- If you have a newspaper format on your word processing software, you can create a wonderful Christmas letter with columns, etc.

- Enlist the talents and ideas of your children and spouse and delegate: one person could design a border around the letter; one could find a quote to include; one could help by typing the letter; one could select art work (clip art is available at print shops).

- Photocopy the letter on festive red or green paper. Add photos, which can be copied with your letter.

- Address and send your Christmas letter!

> *The means to gain happiness is to throw out from oneself, like a spider, in all directions an adhesive web of love, and to catch in it all that comes.*
> — Leo Tolstoy

"Gratitude Is a Memory of the Heart"

Start the tradition of writing thank-you notes for Christmas gifts. In your child's stocking, include a box of colorful thank-you notes and stamps so he or she can express appreciation to grandparents, aunts and uncles, or friends for gifts received at Christmas.

CHAPTER SIX

Christmas Stockings

The Legend of St. Nicholas & the First Christmas Stockings

There are many stories surrounding the benevolent activities of Saint Nicholas, but one of those legends is said to be the origin of our custom of hanging stockings by the chimney on Christmas Eve.

Nicholas was an actual person born in the fourth century in Asia Minor. He devoted his life to giving and doing good deeds and became a priest and bishop at a young age. Since his parents had died early, Nicholas was left a fortune, which he spent mainly in giving to the poor and needy.

In one story Nicholas saved the three daughters of an impoverished nobleman. The nobleman's wife died and in his grief he made bad business decisions and lost everything, even his castle. Thus he and his daughters had to move to a peasant cottage. Since he couldn't provide doweries for them or even take care of them, it looked as though he would be forced to sell them into slavery.

Hearing of the family's plight, Nicholas rode to their home that night and tossed three bags of gold in the window, which landed in the daughters' stockings hanging by the chimney to dry. With the doweries, the girls married and lived happily ever after. So the custom evolved of children hanging up their stockings, or in some countries putting out their shoes, in hopes that St. Nicholas would fill them.

How To Make a Storytelling Stocking for Your Child

- First make or purchase a medium-sized to large stocking. You could make the stocking with material taken from a favorite blanket, quilt, or other memorable item.

- Sew 24 thin ribbons on the outside of the stocking.

- Inside the stocking, place mementos, which could be anything from the child's first rattle to a Cub Scout award or a souvenir of a memorable trip.

- Every day, beginning on the first of December, let your child pull one of the items out of the stocking, and tie it to one of the brightly colored ribbons on the outside. As he does, tell the story of the item and its significance.

- The number of empty ribbons tells the number of days until Christmas. When Christmas Day arrives, the stocking is empty and ready to be filled with treats and surprises. And in the process, your child has learned a lot of his "history" and special little family stories. As he grows, he will want to tell the stories, and you can change the mementos each year.[4]

Stocking Stuffers

*D*on't wait until the last minute to purchase stocking stuffers when prices are high and time is short. Look year round for great little gifts like:

- For kids: a small magnifying glass for stimulating curiosity, personalized pencils, a tiny compass, a special Christmas ornament with the child's name on it, a box of thank-you notes, bubble-blowing liquid, a package of stick-on fluorescent stars for his bedroom ceiling.

- For moms, aunts, and grandmoms: fragrant soaps in pretty shapes, perfumed talc in travel size, a fresh new holiday kitchen towel.

- For dads, uncles, and gramps: a much-wanted tool, a small Swiss army knife, a stick of summer sausage, holiday socks.

- For all: fruit, nuts, and special treats.

CHAPTER SEVEN

Christmas Around The World

Christmas is celebrated differently in countries all over the world. In Mexico, the holiday season lasts from December 16 to January 6. People walk in a procession called "La Posada" and then friends are invited in for refreshments and to break a "pinata," a papier-maché figure filled with candy and little gifts.[5]

The community tree-lighting ceremony, observed by many small towns and cities, and even the White House in Washington, DC, began in Germany, where it was called the "Bescherung."

In France, families celebrate when the Christmas yule log is brought into the home. After sprinkling the log with wine, the father lights it in the fireplace.

In Australia and Hawaii, people often go on a picnic on Christmas Day because it is warm there in December.

In Norway, church bells ring all over the country at four o'clock in the afternoon on Christmas Eve. This rings in the Christmas holiday.

In Sweden, on December 13, families celebrate Saint Lucia Day. The oldest daughter of the family, dressed in a white gown with a bright red sash and a crown of evergreens decked with candles, plays the part of Lucia, the Queen of Lights. She brings special holiday treats and coffee to her parents.

"Is There Room in Your Inn?"

Here's an adaption of the Latin American Posada tradition that a family we know celebrates year after year, to their children's delight. Early in December, the Snowbarger family puts up a nativity scene, but without the Baby Jesus figure in the manger. At bedtime on Christmas Eve, all the lights in the house are turned out and everyone is given a little candle.

Dad is the innkeeper. Mom and the children go around to the bedroom doors (while Dad moves quickly from room to room), knocking and asking, "Is there room in your inn?"

Repeatedly the answer comes back: "No, no room here." Finally the children get to the living room where the innkeeper answers, "Yes, there's room here!" They all go in and place the Baby Jesus figure in the manger. Then bowing down, they sing, "O Come, Let Us Adore Him!"

Instead of hanging stockings on the mantelpiece, this family follows the quaint Latin American tradition of putting out their shoes by the bedroom door, filled with straw. The Wise Men's camels come by during the night, eat the straw, and then fill the empty shoes with candy for the children.

IDEA: Adapt a Christmas tradition from another country or from your own ethnic heritage to an activity you could do in your family. Have a night of celebrating Christmas with a meal or treat from that culture, and read a Christmas story from that land. The public library is a great resource for Christmas stories and customs from all around the world.

International Flair

*O*ne of the best ways not only to share your customs but to learn about Christmas customs from other countries is to invite an international student from a local university to celebrate Christmas with your family or to spend a weekend in your home during the month of December. The student gets to learn firsthand about

American customs and doesn't have to be alone in the dormitory for the holidays, as so many are. You and your family benefit from making a new friend and learning about the student's life, culture, and customs.

Friendship Tablecloth

This is fun to use when international guests come to share holiday or other meals throughout the year. The tablecloth can be of simple muslin or other solid fabric. After the meal, sketch around your guest's handprint on the tablecloth. Later, sew in bright embroidery thread around the handprint, and stitch the student's name and country beside it. The international "Friendship Tablecloth" can be brought out and enjoyed each holiday with its record of foreign guests with whom the family has shared the joy of Christmas through the years.

> *A friend is a present you give yourself.*
> — **Anonymous**

A First Christmas for Zhu Hong

One Christmas season we were in Maine, two thousand miles away from the family and friends with whom we usually enjoyed holiday activities. With no prospects of any visitors from back home, and knowing few people in the town in which we lived, the whole family was a little blue. One day during the week before Christmas I decided to call the University of Southern Maine's international students' office to see if there was a foreign student who had no plans for the holidays.

I explained what I was looking for to the receptionist, a girl with a distinctly Chinese accent. I asked, "Would you know of a student who would like to spend Christmas weekend with an American family?"

"Oh, I do," she said. "I will come! I would be in the dormitory by myself, for everyone is going home, and my family is ten thousand miles away!"

So the Friday before Christmas my children and I drove into Portland to pick up Zhu Hong, a petite, dark-haired girl from Shanghai. A freshman Economics major, one of the top students from her country, Zhu Hong had been in America for over a semester, yet she had never been in an American home. Having grown up in Communist China, she was excited to celebrate her first Christmas, and met us at the door of her dorm, lips smiling and eyes sparkling.

After her arrival at our house, our children asked Zhu Hong if she would like to go ice skating with them on the town's outdoor rink. She had never been on a pair of ice skates in her life, but was eager to try the sport. Bundled up warmly, and with my skates over her shoulder, off they all went.

Later that day, we made our traditional holiday "Sprinkle Cookies" together, and Zhu Hong helped me chop vegetables as I prepared our Christmas Eve buffet. Moments later, singing and laughter chimed in from the family room as our daughter Alison taught her how to play several Christmas carols on the piano.

After the meal that night, Zhu Hong joined us in our family traditions of candlelighting, caroling, and reading the story of the first Christmas from the Bible.

The next morning, after opening her stocking and presents and enjoying our Christmas brunch, Zhu Hong joined us for a walk in the fresh snow. Then she surprised us with a full-length video of life in Shanghai and Beijing which she had filmed and narrated before leaving her homeland. In the film, she showed us her friends inside the university dorms, the bustling city streets crowded with bicycles, scenes from her college dance, and the beautiful Chinese countryside. Although she had had the video for months, we were the first Americans Zhu Hong got to share it with. She then presented us with gifts from China as a bond of friendship.

As we sat around the warm fireplace playing games Christmas night, I thought how full and rich this at-first lonely holiday season had become, how our traditions bloomed with new meaning when we shared them with a friend from across the world, and how Zhu Hong's excitement about the "first Christmas" became ours!

De-stressing the Holiday

For many women, the holidays are the most stressful, exhausting time of the year. Here are some ways to prevent holiday stress:

- Avoid getting so busy that you stop exercising. If you walk or exercise daily, keep it up and you'll have the energy and cheerful attitude to enjoy the holidays!

- Avoid perfectionism, especially wishful fantasies about having the "perfect" house or decorations and unrealistic expectations about how it will be when the kids are back from college or the extended family arrives from out of town.

- Quick-clean before company descends on your house and save the thorough housecleaning for after Christmas when the tree has been taken down and company has left.

- Trade off for the help you need. Swap babysitting chores with a friend while each of you do Christmas errands; ask your teenager or one in the neighborhood to help you cook, serve, and clean up for a party.

- If you have to force the majority of the family to observe a tradition, reevaluate and ask: "Does this activity bring real pleasure, or is it just something we feel like we have to do?" Be willing to open your hand and let a tradition go, and often a new one will evolve in its place.

- Take fifteen to twenty minutes to focus on the reason for the season of Christmas. Sit down by the tree and read an inspirational Christmas story.

Two Great Family De-Stressers:

A Holiday Puzzle

*O*n a table where it can be left out, set a new puzzle of 500-1,000 pieces. Make it a goal to have the whole picture completed by Christmas Eve (or New Year's Eve). As family members are in and out, the puzzle provides little slow-down spots of time to gather, put a few pieces of the puzzle in, and chat. When visitors stop by, they too can enjoy putting together "a piece of the puzzle."

Classic Christmas Movie Night

Gather the family together with take-out pizza or Chinese food. Snuggle up in sleeping bags and quilts and have on hand plenty of popcorn and cider. Watch a favorite classic Christmas movie video such as: *It's a Wonderful Life*, *Meet Me in St. Louis*, *Miracle on 34th Street*, or *White Christmas*.

> ### Day Before Christmas
> We have been helping with the cake
> And licking out the pan,
> And wrapping up our packages
> As neatly as we can.
> And we have hung our stockings up
> Beside the open grate,
> And now there's nothing more to do
> Except to wait!
> — **Marchette Chute**

The Plastic Baby In the Manger

It was to be our last Christmas in our Cedar Ridge home, the house in which we had raised our four children and welcomed grandchildren, friends, and our "adopted" college kids for decades of Christmases. I had gone all-out to decorate the house to perfection, and our children and their kids were coming to our house immediately after Sunday school on Christmas Day.

Throughout the house, everything had a theme: there were gorgeous butterflies with matching ribbons on the Christmas tree. Our collector's nativity scene was set up, and ribbon-bedecked candleholders and lights glowed everywhere in the house. This was our last Christmas here, and we wanted it to be special.

When our son David arrived with his family, we hugged at the door. Suddenly Luke, their two-and-a-half-year old, breezed by us all and raced for the nativity set in the family room. Luke took the Italian-made Baby Jesus right out of the manger scene and hid him behind the stable as we watched in amusement. Then he pulled out of a little homemade box something all wrapped up in a baby blue cloth and whacked it down right in the middle of the manger — a celluloid plastic doll that didn't even match the other nativity characters and was twice the size of Mary and Joseph. This baby Jesus didn't fit in at all.

At first I thought, "Oh, my goodness, you've ruined the whole thing!" But then Luke looked up at me with his eyes shining and said, "Isn't my Baby Jesus beautiful?" as he admired his plastic doll in the manger. My heart melted.

And from that Christmas to this day, Luke's plastic Baby Jesus is our baby in the manger (while the ornate Italian Baby Jesus is put away). And although he's six-two and in college now, every year at Christmas when we put out the manger scene with Luke's celluloid Baby Jesus, we think of the wonder of a two-year-old and the memory of that Christmas so long ago.

How much more important it is for things that are dear to our children and grandchildren to be a part of our Christmas instead of having everything be matched and decorator-perfect!

— Dorothy Shellenberger

CHAPTER EIGHT

Turning Family Treasures Into Family Traditions

Make A Memory Wreath Ornament

When my mother died, my sisters and I faced the unpleasant task of taking care of her personal effects. When we came across the gold brocade dress that Mom had worn to all three of our weddings, the tears flowed. We couldn't bear to give or throw away the special dress! So I took swatches of the fabric and wrapped them around three-inch curtain rings, fashioning wreath ornaments for my tree, and for those of my sisters, and even their children. What priceless gifts these ornaments became!

You can use material from any significant source to make the Memory Wreath Ornaments: a wedding gown, a baby's christening gown, a bridesmaid's dress, your child's sports suit or Scout uniform, or any outgrown outfit.

Memory Wreath Ornaments make a Christmas tree so much more than a dressed-up evergreen! With a little care and imagination, your tree can remind you of the blessings of family and friends, happy events from days gone by. By replacing standard Christmas balls and store-bought decorations with family treasures, you can create your own "Memory Tree."

Fabric Wreath Ornament: A Memory Worth Making

Materials:

- A 3-inch wooden Kirsch curtain ring with eyelet screw. Check hardware or discount stores.
- Memory material 2 1/2 inches wide. The length will depend on the weight and texture of the fabric.
- Matching lace or other edging 3/4 inch wide and twice as long as material.
- A 13-inch ribbon 5/8 inch wide.
- Matching thread.

Directions:

1. Turn material edge under approximately 1/4 inch and machine stitch lace or edging to right side of both long edges.
2. Fold material in half lengthwise and machine stitch wrong sides of material together to make a 1-inch wide casing.

3. Cut through wooden ring near eyelet screw. A saber saw or band saw works well for this job.
4. Slide the casing over the ring at the cut. Distribute the ruffles evenly around the ring.
5. Tie bow at screw.
6. Experiment with the length and width for various types of fabric.[6]

More Gifts That Money Can't Buy

Family History

A gift of the family history is a treasure money can't buy. When an old person in a family dies, it's like a library of memories and history has burned down. Before that happens, spend a little while visiting with a grandparent or other elderly relative. Don't forget to take a cassette recorder with a blank tape to record the stories, share a plate of cookies, and enjoy your time together! Here are some ways to get the stories going:

- Ask your relative to make a "memory map" — a little sketch of the floor plan of the earliest house he or she remembers living in. Then ask questions about events that happened there, like: "Who were the people who lived there with you?" "What were your pastimes?" "How did you spend Christmas as a family?"

- Look around the room or the attic and bring in a special object from the past — an old rifle or sewing machine that belonged to the great-grandparent, an article of clothing, or an award, and have the relative talk about its meaning.

- With the stories that are generated, write a short booklet of "Heritage History" about your family. You can video or audio tape the oral history as the relative shares it, and make copies of the tape for members of the family.

Christmas Placemats

Cut pieces of Christmas fabric — red and green country print, gingham, or other — in 12" X 20" inch rectangles. Hem the edge if uneven or ragged. Then laminate the fabric at an educational supply store or by placing clear contact paper covering both sides — and you have an easy-to-make holiday placemat.

Tips On Giving From Your Kitchen

- Give something that can be frozen by the recipient. Because some people get so many food gifts, they appreciate being able to freeze some and enjoy them at another time.

- Give a breakfast item of food. A pan of cinnamon rolls or coffee cake that can be eaten for Christmas morning breakfast is always appreciated.

- If you are making pies for gifts or for gatherings, make your pie crust ahead of time (before Thanksgiving even). Then all you have to do is thaw out the crust, put in the filling, and — voila! — fresh, homemade pie!

Give to the world the best that you have, And the best will come back to you.
— **Madeline Bridges**

One Christmas Eve

*I*t was 4:00 p.m. on December 24th, and my wife Ruby's words rang in my ears. "Birthdays are wonderful, but Christmas is that special time to remember each other." My heart ached because she always did. On this festive eve, I was worried.

Christmas Eve at the industrial plant where I worked was a special time. Co-workers glowed. There were handshakes and hugs as "MERRY CHRISTMAS" rang up and down the aisles. Joy filled the air.

It was an especially jubilant time for us working the 3:00 until 11:00 p.m. shift. We were permitted to leave work at 7:00 p.m. — four hours earlier. An eagerly anticipated evening off, these were precious hours to spend with family and loved ones.

Yet, this Christmas Eve I was troubled. Even though work conditions had slumped since September, as contracts terminated and layoffs began, I was caught napping. Overnight I was demoted from highly-skilled machine operator to floor sweeper. Suddenly, financial obligations soared as income dwindled. Now, it was Christmas Eve and I didn't have money to buy Ruby a Christmas gift. We'd been married thirteen years, and I had always managed a gift, even during my wartime duty overseas with the Army. This year it was different, and I was desolate.

This was the time before easy credit. I scolded myself for poor planning, and chided myself for being short-sighted. I should have sacrificed and saved through a Christmas Club at the local bank.

To ease my tensions, I swept the floor vigorously. I dug into corners, into nooks and crannies. I felt a warm pride about my area. I always felt good about a job well-done, no matter how menial. One by one, co-workers complimented me about the area. "It sparkles, Oscar," they yelled.

As I pushed the broom I prayed. I asked God to forgive me and to help Ruby understand. I asked Him to ease her disappointment and show me a way to make it up to her. Still, that wouldn't erase the fact that I had failed. I knew she had scrimped and saved and would remember. I was ashamed.

The evening passed quickly and my thoughts remained troubled. It was 7:00 p.m., and time to go home.

I was placing my broom in the closet when I felt a hand on my shoulder. I turned and faced Al, a small dark-haired co-worker, from the machine area where I formerly worked. Al was a highly skilled mechanic whose years of company service prevented a layoff or downgrade.

"Oscar," he said, "your area always looks nice, but tonight it's tops! We miss you being on the machine, and we want you to have a Merry Christmas!"

Al reached and pressed something in my hand. I looked and saw two new, crisp, ten-dollar bills, more than enough for Ruby's gift. It was from co-workers who were not required to be so thoughtful. My eyes glistened as Al thoughtfully looked away. I swallowed hard and thanked him.

I left work and boarded a bus, my mind racing with thoughts concerning a gift for Ruby. Then, on that noisy, crowded bus, I closed my eyes and thanked God for touching the hearts of my co-workers and answering my prayers. Joy to the World! It would be a Merry Christmas, I was certain of that![7]

— Oscar H. Greene

The Lollipop Tree

Kids are always asking, "How many days till Christmas?" For the last twelve days before Christmas make a "Lollipop Tree," and they can count the days. Cut a white piece of posterboard or heavy cardboard in the shape of a big Christmas tree, and mount it on their bedroom door. Decorate the cardboard with a colored tape border and write their individual names at the top. Buy strips of lollipops for ease in making rows.

For the base of the tree, cut the bottom half of a disposable paper cup and decorate with foil or red wrapping paper. Tape the base of the tree to the cardboard. Put one lollipop at the top of the cardboard for the point of the tree, and then make strips of lollipops across in rows in the shape of a tree.

Each day until Christmas one lollipop gets to be taken off and eaten. (This can be adapted to any number of days before Christmas.)[8]

CHAPTER NINE

Let's Go A-Caroling

Sometime during the last weeks before Christmas, it's fun to invite a few families, including all the children, for caroling. You can carol in just your neighborhood or at a local nursing home or hospital. What's important is just getting together to sing the wonderful Christmas songs of old and to share the Good News and holiday cheer with people around you.

To feed the hungry carolers, you can:

- Ask each family to bring something for a "potluck" supper.

- Serve snacks like cheese and crackers, fruit, and tiny sandwiches and chips before caroling.

- Serve Christmas cookies when the singers return to your house (see recipes below for "Sprinkle Cookies" and delicious, hot "Caroler's Punch").

Sing a Carol & Hear the Story — "Silent Night"

*O*ne December 24, 1818, in the little village of Oberndorf, Austria, the whole town was preparing to come to the Christmas service, the highlight of the season. But the parish priest, Father Joseph Mohr, was worried. The chapel organ was broken, and because of the heavy snowfall, the repairman from the next town could not get there to fix it. The service would be devoid of the beloved Christmas music.

For months he had been wanting to write a new song to express the simplicity and holiness of Christmas, but the words had eluded him. That night, as he sat at his desk pondering what to do about the music, he saw someone struggling through the deep snow to get to his cabin. A woman stood there, explaining that a family from over the mountain had asked that he come to their home that night to bless their first child who had just been born.

Bundling up, the priest started out through the snow and, after several hours of walking, came to the couple's cabin and the most beautiful scene he'd ever laid eyes on. There was the new mother in her bed smiling, as she and the father were looking in the little wooden crib beside her bed that held their newborn son. Father Mohr admired the baby and blessed him and his parents. Then as he trudged home through the silent snow, he thought of the little family and how much it was like the scene in Bethlehem centuries before on the first Christmas night.

The words flowed as joy filled Mohr's heart, and as soon as he arrived home, he wrote them down. That very morning he asked his friend, Franz Gruber, to compose the tune to the song. That evening "Silent Night" was heard for the first time by the little congregation at Oberndorf — with Gruber accompanying on his guitar as both men sang. Originally written for two voices and a guitar, the carol became the most popular Christmas hymn in Europe and America.

Silent Night

Silent night! Holy night!
All is calm, all is bright.
'Round yon Virgin Mother and Child!
Holy Infant, so tender and mild,
Sleep in heavenly peace,
Sleep in heavenly peace.

Silent night! Holy night!
Shepherds quake at the sight!
Glories stream from heaven afar,
Heav'nly hosts sing, "Alleluia!"
Christ, the Savior, is born!
Christ, the Savior, is born!

Silent night! Holy night!
Son of God, love's pure light!
Radiant beams from Thy holy face
With the dawn of redeeming grace,
Jesus, Lord, at Thy birth,
Jesus, Lord, at Thy birth.

— Joseph Mohr and Franz Gruber

There's A Song In the Air...
Caroling Customs

Throughout the ages, singing has been a part of almost every holiday and festival. The custom of singing Christmas carols goes back to the first century, so some of the carols we sing are so old no one knows the author. Most early carols were written in Latin and were sung as part of nativity plays. St. Francis of Assisi was said to encourage his followers in singing at the Christmas season.

Although our Puritan forefathers disapproved of carol singing and merry-making at Christmas, caroling was a beloved pastime that spread across the United States in towns and cities as people sang of "peace on earth, good will to men," to their neighbors, to lonely shut-ins, and to friends. Today the caroling tradition is alive and well in many families and churches as people let their voices ring out with the joy of Christmas.

Reindeer Paths

It must have been a Christmas Eve sometime in the 1940s when my grandparents, George and Barbara Gabbitas, first bundled up their young family and went caroling to their dearest friends and neighbors. I can only imagine the sound of their voices in the cold night air: my grandmother's lilting soprano piercing the darkness, with my grandfather's sure and resonant bass rolling beneath the enthusiastic chime of three children. Silent night, holy night, all is calm, all is bright . . . .

My grandmother had delivered her first child on Christmas Day, 1930, a stillborn baby boy. Perhaps she buried a portion of that Christmas grief every year after in the joyous carols of the season. These were presented as gifts to friends from a family that did not have much else to give.

Christmas Eve caroling became a tradition for the Gabbitas family. Friends eagerly awaited their visits and would often comment that it just didn't feel quite like Christmas until the Gabbitas had sung "Silent Night."

My grandparents' five children eventually married and began families of their own. All spouses and grandchildren unwittingly entered the extended family with an unspoken, unwritten commitment to carol every Christmas Eve for life. Thus, I began my caroling career at the age of ten months and never missed a Christmas Eve singing to a vast collection of friends over the next twenty-four years.

I vividly remember being six and singing at the top of my lungs on someone's front lawn with my eyes cast skyward, believing that the flashing red light I saw among the stars was indeed Rudolph's nose guiding The Sleigh. It was almost too much excitement and wonder for my six-year-old heart to bear, and the magic of that moment branded itself in my memory. How deliciously secure I was — a parent holding each hand, surrounded by aunts and uncles with babies in their arms or a toddler on a hip, swaying with the carol as though it were a lullaby. 'Round yon Virgin, Mother and Child . . . . This was my family.

Too soon I was ten, and Santa and flying reindeer were put to rest. This Christmas, I would join the ranks of grownups and pretend the magic was "real" for the sake of my two young brothers and baby sister. A part of my Christmas was fading and there was nothing to be done about it. All the brightly colored lights outlining roofs and windows and sparkling in trees just didn't seem as vibrant that year. Then, I was huddled with my family against the December chill singing familiar words that suddenly sprang to life in my mind, filling the emptiness with a thing of great wonder. Holy Infant so tender and mild . . . . The magic was real.

I remember Christmas Eves caroling as a teenager, each year marking how our family had grown and changed. It was not a simple task to assemble such a mob on anyone's front lawn. No longer a little family straining to be heard on a winter's night, we were a roving choir with a Christmas Eve errand. Watching their faces as we sang, I considered the lifetime of experiences I shared with cousins that numbered nearly thirty. We had played, laughed, fought, pretended, invented, and dreamed together. Our lives were interwoven like the consonant chords of a sweet carol. And the blend of voices was a sound only a family could create. I was proud to be one of those voices, delivering a gift so full of joy and love — one that I could never offer alone.

I remember the last Christmas before my younger brother left to become a missionary in Peru and feeling that our warm, close-knit family was on the verge of unraveling. There would be another brother missing the following year, then a cousin. We would marry, move away. Grandparents would age and die. Things would never be the same again. Those rich harmonies seemed more precious to me that night than ever before because I knew they would not last forever. Sleep in heavenly peace . . . .

My first Christmas Eve in Oklahoma was a little depressing despite the fact that I was welcomed by loving in-laws and a new family. Here were new and unfamiliar traditions: a soup dinner, a Christmas reading, opening one present on Christmas Eve . . . yet I longed to be surrounded by those voices and people who had shaped my Christmas Eves for as long as I could remember. I called my parents' home long-distance and caught my mother.

"Oh, we were just walking out the door to go caroling. Let us sing 'Silent Night' to you before we go," she said. And as they sang, I was with them, remembering icy nights, our white frosted breath curled heavenward like a family prayer — a solemn benediction at the close of a year. And they were with me, helping me to see beyond my emptiness, helping me find my new home.

Someday I'll have the chance to return and spend a Christmas Eve in my hometown, and when I do, I'll bring my husband and our children with me. We'll huddle together in the December chill and add our voices to the Gabbitas choir. I will kneel on someone's crisp winter grass and point out to my three young sons the path among the stars that flying reindeer might take. I will see the brilliant colors of Christmas lights reflected in their eyes and hear the carol begin anew. Silent night, holy night, all is calm, all is bright. . . .

— Stephanie Russell Sloat

Christmas Sprinkle Cookies

With this cookie dough, you can make several kinds of cookie treats: cut-out sugar cookies (we call ours "Sprinkle Cookies" because of the green and red sprinkles we decorate them with), Stained-Glass Cookies, and the Star of Bethlehem. They are perfect to serve a group of hungry carolers, a gathering of friends, or a school party.

Cut-Out Sugar Cookies

Ingredients:

1 cup butter	2 cups flour
1 cup sugar	1/2 teaspoon baking soda
1 egg	1/2 teaspoon cream of tartar
2 teaspoons vanilla	

Directions: Cream the butter and sugar. Add egg and vanilla and beat well. Sift the dry ingredients and mix to form dough. Refrigerate 2 balls of dough covered until ready to roll out and cut into Christmas cookies. Bake at 350 degrees F until lightly browned; cool and decorate.

Before baking, you can decorate cookies with green or red sprinkles, silver balls, or cinnamon candies. If you decorate after baking, first spread with icing from a tube (store-bought) or pastry bag. Then add sprinkles or other decorations.

Stained-Glass Cookies

These are colorful Christmas cookies which can be used for eating or as ornaments to string on a cookie tree or across a window.

Ingredients:
"Cut-Out Sugar Cookie" recipe
1/3 cup or more crushed colored hard candies

Directions: Separate colors of hard candy and put each color in a zip-lock bag and crush. Preheat oven to 375 degrees F. Make dough according to sugar cookie recipe. After chilling for 2 to 3 hours, roll out dough to 1/8 inch thickness on lightly floured board. Cut out cookies using large Christmas cookie cutters.

Transfer cookies to a foil-lined baking sheet. Using a small cookie cutter of the same shape as the large one, cut out and remove dough from the center of each cookie. Fill the cut-out sections with crushed candy. If using cookies as hanging ornaments, make a hole with the sharp point of a pencil at the top of each cookie for string.

Bake 7 to 9 minutes or until cookies are lightly browned and candy melted. Slide foil off baking sheets, and when cool, carefully loosen cookies from foil.

CHAPTER TEN

Holiday Hospitality

Our house is open, Lord, to thee;

Come in, and share our Christmas tree!

We've made each nook and corner bright,

Burnished with yellow candlelight.

But light that never burns away

Is only thine, Lord Jesus, stay,

Shine on us now, our Christmas Cheer —

Fill with Thy flame our whole New Year![9]

— Luci Shaw

Easy Ways to Entertain at Christmas

*O*ne of the best parts of the Christmas season is inviting friends —young and old — into our homes to share a cup of Christmas tea and some holiday cookies, visiting with neighbors we often miss during normal hectic school and work weeks, or asking another family over for a warm night of visiting and eating.

In whatever form, traditions of hospitality are special expressions of Christmas love you can find in your own backyard or family room. Holiday gatherings don't have to be large or elaborate — hot cherry cobbler and coffee, a favorite dessert from your kitchen, or even store-bought gingerbread men, can form the backdrop for a memorable occasion. Here are easy ways to extend hospitality to those right around you:

Neighborhood Cookie Exchange

$\mathcal{A}$ cookie exchange is a great idea for a winter neighborhood block party (or a get-together with your circle of friends). It provides a wonderful opportunity to chat in a busy season during which neighbors might otherwise only catch a glimpse of each other pulling in and out of their driveways. If the tasks are shared, no one is overwhelmed with preparations.

Two families who serve as "hosts" can make invitations on a sheet of white paper — computer designed or handwritten. (If your kids like to create on-screen, they might love to take over this part!) The invitations can be copied on bright red or green paper. Children can decorate them with crayons or stickers, and hand deliver them.

Each family brings a batch of two dozen of their favorite homemade cookies, and the recipe, which are all put out on the dining table on trays. That way everyone goes home with a variety of different cookies. Punch and cookie-tasting follow.

A Newcomer's Christmas

It was three weeks before Christmas. We had just moved to Oklahoma City with our three children, the boys both under five years old, and three-week-old baby Alison in my arms. With no family or friends in the area, I busied myself unpacking boxes and trying to decorate the house between feedings, diaper washing, and housework. All three of the children had just come through a bad bout with bronchitis, and cabin fever had set in for them. Cranky and bored, they longed to get out and meet kids in the neighborhood. They were tired of hearing me read the same books, and thought it would never be Christmas when their grandparents would come.

As for me, I was feeling isolated and a little blue in the long hours my husband was working at the retail store across town. I was still trying to find my way to the

> *Each Christmas*
> *we share*
> *With friends both*
> *far and near*
> *Makes our*
> *years together*
> *So memorable*
> *and dear.*
> — Anonymous

doctor's office and grocery store. If there just were someone to call, or if I knew somebody in the neighborhood who had kids too.

Suddenly there was a knock at my door. A mother who looked about my age smiled and held out a hand-made invitation to her "Neighborhood Christmas Coffee" that Saturday. With two little ones in tow, she said, "Bring your children, too, and a treat or bread if you have time."

As a newcomer, that Saturday coffee was the highlight of my first holiday season in a strange new environment. The country-print-covered table was filled with coffee rings and loaves of warm nut bread each neighbor had brought. The smell of hot cider and coffee laced the room as four other mothers and I sat around the fireplace and talked about our kids — between us there were fourteen! Through the window I could see them bundled up, playing in the backyard. The idea emerged to start a neighborhood play group so they, and we, could get to know each other better and have some time out of the house in the winter.

The warmth and friendliness I experienced was one of the best Christmas gifts I received that year, and new friendships were started that day that lasted after we moved away and even years later when our children were out of high school and beyond.

*Villagers all,
this frosty tide,
Let your doors
swing open wide,
Though wind may
follow, and
snow beside,
Yet draw us in by
your fire to bide;
Joy shall be yours in
the morning! . . .*
— Kenneth Grahame

CHAPTER ELEVEN

Light a Candle — Home for the Holidays

Candles, Candles, Shining Bright

One of the oldest and richest symbols of Christmas is the candle, lit and shining to symbolize the glory of the bright light in the Bethlehem stable that first Christmas night, and to signify Christ as the Light of the World.

Whether they are candles burning in the front of a Christmas church service, tall, thin tapers in the middle of a Christmas Eve table, or single candles shining inside a green wreath in each window of a New England house, candles are an integral part of holiday festivities all over the world.

Lighting Your House

- Arrange your favorite candlesticks around a bed of evergreen boughs. Add a bow to each candlestick and set a deep green candle in each.

- Get a little string of tiny white twinkle lights and tack around your child's bedroom window.

- On Christmas Eve after supper, give each family member a white candle in a stiff cardboard disk to catch candledrips. Turn out all the lights except the Christmas tree lights, and let each person share a favorite Christmas memory or what he or she is especially grateful for. To close, with candles lit, sing "Silent Night."

A Tender Christmas

$\mathbb{E}$ach year we had enjoyed a big celebration at our house with my parents, the in-laws, aunts, and our children — complete with a delicious, festive meal and watching the children open their gifts. But this year it was going to be different. My father had fallen and broken his hip on December 6. He would be home from the hospital but bedfast on Christmas Eve. My in-laws were sick, and I too had been ill.

On Christmas Eve, we went over to my parents' apartment after dinner. I took a candle for each person, and after we had gathered together, turned out the lights and had each person share two things they were thankful for and something they wished or hoped for.

I shared first, gratitude for my father's place in my life and for all the Christmases my uncle had spent with us before his death. My mother began to talk, and then broke into tears. Next was my Aunt Betsy, whose husband had passed away just after Thanksgiving. Then my Dad, who expressed gratefulness to God for being home with the family after his surgery. My Auntie May, age ninety, was thankful for her long life and hoped for health to the end of her days.

My teenage son shifted uncomfortably, cleared his throat, and shared from his heart. Then my fourteen-year-old daughter spoke. By this time there was a circle of light from our candles. We began to sing familiar Christmas carols there in the darkness. Then slowly Auntie May and Aunt Betsy began to reminisce about the days when my parents courted secretly at May's house. It was a wonderful way to close the evening. It made me think of precious gold beads being slipped onto the necklace of time like the memories that link us together as family members. And although the year had held difficult times, it was the most tender Christmas we've ever had.

Sharing a Christmas Classic

> Life holds no sweeter thing than this:
> To teach a little child the tale most loved on earth
> And watch the wonder deepen in his eyes
> There while you tell him of the Christ Child's birth;
> The while you tell him of shepherds and a song,
> Of gentle drowsy beast and fragrant hay
> On which that starlit night in Bethlehem
> God's tiny Son and His young mother lay . . .[10]
>
> — Adelaide Love

One of the loveliest and easiest traditions is to put your favorite Christmas books in a big basket tied up with a bright holiday bow and set it by the Christmas tree to be enjoyed by all. Having the basket of Christmas classics close by, you'll be encouraged to sit down and read a story to your child. You may even find your teenager sitting down when no one is looking and rereading one of his childhood favorites. You can have a "turn off the TV night," curl up around a crackling fireplace, and take turns reading Christmas stories after supper. And longer stories or books, like Raphael, The Herald Angel or The Story of the Other Wise Man can be read a chapter a night during the holidays.

To build your own collection of Christmas classics, go to book fairs and used book sales and you'll find some great bargains. Also peruse your local library for Christmas collections that can be checked out and placed temporarily in your basket. Here are some treasured stories and books you won't want to miss:

Alcott, Louisa May, "A Christmas Dream and How It Came True"
Allsburg, Chris, The Polar Express
Andersen, Hans Christian, "The Fir Tree"
Appel, David, and Hudson, Merle, Raphael, The Herald Angel
Cleary, Beverly, "Ramona and the Three Wise Persons"
Dickens, Charles, A Christmas Carol
Hegg, Tom, A Cup of Christmas Tea
Henry, O., "The Gift of the Magi"
MacDonald, George, The Gifts of the Christ Child
Moore, Clement Clarke, "The Night Before Christmas"
Robinson, Barbara, The Best Christmas Pageant Ever
Van Dyke, Henry, The Story of the Other Wise Man

The Christmas Tissue

A few days prior to Christmas in 1982, my wife, Margaret, and I heard from our church that a family in the nearby town of Yukon, Oklahoma, was experiencing difficulties. In fact, their kitchen cupboards were bare. We headed for the grocery store, and found ourselves a little carried away as we went up and down the aisles putting cartons and boxes in the basket. There were corn chips, milk, large bottles of soft drinks, cookies, as well as healthier staple foods, meat, and paper products.

Snowy Christmases are unusual in Oklahoma, but that night there was a heavy snow covering the ground as we unloaded the groceries and the family's older children helped us cart the sacks in.

As we chatted with the mother and father, the four young children were busy inspecting the sacks and putting produce in the refrigerator, cereal boxes and other food away in the kitchen cabinets. Suddenly little ten-year-old Charlie bounded from the kitchen with a four-pack of toilet tissue held high in his left hand.

"Look, mom, toilet paper!" The mother and father shot a glance at us, with a rather sheepish look on their faces, as Charlie skipped toward the bathroom to put away the tissue.

That was a memorable Christmas. I cannot remember what gifts we exchanged among the family. Today, several years later, I have no idea whether I received a tie, new slacks, or what. And I cannot remember what I gave to Margaret, or what we gave to our daughters. Nor can I recall what special Christmas musical services we might have attended. However, I will always remember that scene of Charlie skipping through the house with a pack of toilet tissue held high!

— Dee Stribling

The Joy of Giving

Somehow not only for Christmas
But all the long year through,
The joy that you give to others
Is the joy that comes back to you.
And the more you spend in blessing
The poor and lonely and sad
The more of your heart's possessing
Returns to make you glad.

— John Greenleaf Whittier

Giving and serving together brings a family or friends closer together and helps to create an appreciation of the true spirit of Christmas.

Food Basket

Put a small basket in the center of your dining room table and encourage each person, big and small, to do little odd jobs and earn extra money to put in the basket. Each family member contributes something, no matter how small. Then just before Christmas, parents and children go to the grocery store to select items for a holiday food basket for a less fortunate family in the community.

Salvation Army & Project Angel Tree

Each of these is a Gift-Wish Tree in which you select a child's name, buy the gifts, and return them to the Salvation Army or hand-deliver to the child. Project Angel Trees has the names of children of prison inmates who otherwise would be forgotten at Christmas, and can be contacted at P. O. Box 17500, Washington, D.C. 20041.

CHAPTER TWELVE

The Christmas Story

*A*bout this time Caesar Augustus, the Roman Emperor, decreed that a census should be taken throughout the nation. (This census was taken when Quinirius was governor of Syria.)

Everyone was required to return to his ancestral home for this registration. And because Joseph was a member of the royal line, he had to go to Bethlehem in Judea, King David's ancient home — journeying there from the Galilean village of Nazareth. He took with him Mary, his fiancée, who was obviously pregnant by this time.

And while they were there, the time came for her baby to be born; and she gave birth to her first child, a son. She wrapped him in a blanket and laid him in a manger, because there was no room for them in the village inn.

That night some shepherds were in the fields outside the village, guarding their flocks of sheep.

Suddenly an angel appeared among them, and the landscape shone bright with the glory of the Lord. They were badly frightened, but the angel reassured them.

"Don't be afraid!" he said. "I bring you the most joyful news ever announced, and it is for everyone! The Savior — yes, the Messiah, the Lord — has been born tonight in Bethlehem! How will you recognize him? You will find a baby wrapped in a blanket, lying in a manger!"

Suddenly, the angel was joined by a vast host of others — the armies of heaven — praising God:

"Glory to God in the highest heaven," they sang, "and peace on earth for all those pleasing him."

When this great army of angels had returned again to heaven, the shepherds said to each other, "Come on! Let's go to Bethlehem! Let's see this wonderful thing that has happened, which the Lord has told us about."

They ran to the village and found their way to Mary and Joseph. And there was the baby, lying in the manger. The shepherds told everyone what had happened and what the angel had said to them about this child.

All who heard the shepherds' story expressed astonishment, but Mary quietly treasured these things in her heart and often thought about them.

Then the shepherds went back again to their fields and flocks, praising God for the visit of the angels, and because they had seen the child, just as the angel had told them.

— Luke 2:1-20 TLB

Endnotes

[1] Originally published in *Listening to the Littlest* (Norwalk, CT: C.R. Gibson, Publisher, 1984). Used by permission.

[2] My thanks to Laura Neely of Dallas, Texas, for sharing the directions for the "Apple Santas" that her grandmother always made for their family and Laura makes for hers every year.

[3] Originally published in *Guideposts*, December, 1994, p. 21. Used by permission.

[4] Excerpted from Posy Lough's "The Posy Collection," P. O. Box 394, Simsbury, CT 06070.

[5] Adapted from *World Book Encyclopedia*, Vol. 3 (Chicago: World Book-Childcraft International, Inc., 1981).

[6] Excerpted from *Christmas Decorations: Turning Treasures into Traditions*. For more craft ideas and historic cross-stitch kits, write "The Posy Collection," P. O. Box 394, Simsbury, CT 06070.

[7] Originally published by *The Gem*, December 22, 1985.

[8] My thanks to Louise Tucker Jones for sharing this craft idea.

[9] From a greeting card published by World Wide Publications, 1303 Hennepin Avenue, Minneapolis, MN 55403. Used by permission.

[10] Used by permission of Heartland Samplers, 9947 Valley View Road, Eden Prairie, MN 55344.

OTHER BOOKS
BY CHERI FULLER

Motivating Your Kids
From Crayons to Career

Home-Life
The Key to Your Child's
Success at School

Available from your local bookstore.

About the Author

Cheri Fuller, born in Dallas, Texas, was the fourth of six children. Home was the place where something interesting was always happening. Even as a small child, she remembers the art time, nature walks, backyard games, and playing school at home with her sisters. Because of these experiences, she learned to read before starting school. In the course of family life, she also began writing — long letters to grandparents and to an uncle who lived in Alaska, poems for birthday cards, and verses for special occasions.

Cheri has had extensive experience in teaching English and creative writing. She taught freshman composition at the university level, and inner city catch-up programs for disadvantaged youth, public junior high, private college preparatory school, Christian elementary, junior high, and high school.

She also taught history and world geography. She has privately tutored, team-taught, and written curriculum.

Through her academic experience she developed a concern for the sliding academic skills she saw in the classroom and wanted to use her experience to help parents provide an environment supportive to learning. This led her to research the causes and solutions to the school problems and to write a book for parents. She teaches workshops for parent groups and PTA's on topics such as learning style, encouraging reading and writing skills, and other topics, and teaches in the classroom young authors' workshops to encourage their writing skills.

Cheri holds a bachelor's degree in English, history, and secondary education, and a Master's degree in English Literature from Baylor University in Waco, Texas. She and her husband Holmes have three children: Justin, Chris and Alison.

To contact Cheri Fuller,
write:

Cheri Fuller
P. O. Box 770493
Oklahoma City, Oklahoma 73177